W9-AAX-748

natural disasters

FIRST RESPONSE: BY LAND

Aileen Weintraub

Children's Press®
A Division of Scholastic Inc.
New York / Toronto / London / Auckland / Sydney
Mexico City / New Delhi / Hong Kong
Danbury, Connecticut

Book Design: Erica Clendening
Contributing Editor: Geeta Sobha
Photo Credits: Cover © Mark Wilson/Getty Images; pg. © Chris Graythen/Getty Images; pg. 7 © Justin Sullivan/Getty Images; pg. 8 © Omar Torres/AFP/Getty Images; pg. 11 © Mario Tama/Getty Images; pg. 12 Marko Georgiev/Images; pg. 14 © NyxoLno Cangemi/U.S. Coast Guard via Getty Images; pg. 15 © Jensen Walker/Getty Images; pg. 18 © Mark Wilson/Getty Images; pg. 18 © Menahem Kahana/AFP/Getty Images; pg. 21 © Liz Hafalia/San Francisco Chronicle/Corbis; pg. 22 © Alex Wong/Getty Images; pg. 23 © Justin Sullivan/Getty Images; pg. 24 © Jewel Samad/AFP/Getty Images; pg. 26 © Mario Tama/Getty Images; pg. 28 © Andrea Booher/FEMA News Photo/Liaison Agency; pg. 31 © Andrea Decanini/Reuters/Corbis; pg. 35 © Andy Nelson/The Christian Science Monitor via Getty Images; pg. 36 © Stan Honda/AFP/Getty Images; pg. 41 © Eric Feferberg/AFP/Getty Images

Library of Congress Cataloging-in-Publication Data:

Weintraub, Aileen, 1973-
   First response : by land / Aileen Weintraub.
   p. cm. — (Natural disasters)
   Includes index.
   ISBN-10: 0-531-12433-9 (lib. bdg.)   0-531-18719-5 (pbk.)
   ISBN-13: 978-0-531-12433-8 (lib. bdg.) 978-0-531-18719-7 (pbk.)
     1. Emergency management—Juvenile literature. 2. Disaster relief—Juvenile literature. I. Title. II. Series: Natural disasters (Children's Press)

HV551.2.W45 2007
363.34'8-dc22
                                 2006011893

CONTENTS

First responders, such as police officers, give speedy aid to victims in the wake of natural disasters.

The date is September 21, 2005. The governors of Texas, Louisiana, and Florida order residents to evacuate their homes. The weather centers are on alert. Hurricane Rita, a category five hurricane, is blowing into the Gulf of Mexico. Winds are up to 175 miles (282 kilometers) per hour. This is the most powerful hurricane to ever enter the Gulf of Mexico.

Within two days, Rita breaks levees in New Orleans that were already damaged by Hurricane Katrina, which hit just weeks earlier. The storm finally reaches land on September 24. Strong winds uproot trees and flatten houses. Power lines are blown down, and buildings are reduced to rubble. Acres of rice and sugarcane farmland are flooded. Floods also drown thousands of cattle. When the storm is over, many people are injured. Some are homeless.

Who will help the victims of this natural disaster? The speediest help will come from emergency workers called first responders. They know there will be a lot of devastation to places hit by Hurricane Rita. They also know that they have no time to waste once the storm is over. The first few hours–even minutes–after a natural disaster are critical. That's when the most lives are saved.

The National Guard races into the devastated areas to conduct search and rescue. They pull stranded residents out of flooded areas to safety. Engineers and military police work together. They remove fallen trees and other debris that get in the way of rescue efforts. The American Red Cross rushes to open new shelters for hurricane victims. Here, people will be given food, water, and medical attention. Hundreds of doctors and nurses are called into the area to provide medical assistance.

The first responders know that their reaction time can be a matter of life or death. How do they go about helping victims? First responders need special training and specific equipment to do their jobs. Read on to find out about the first responders who provide help on land.

Powerful hurricanes can cause deadly coastal floods if proper measures are not taken to prevent them.

Rescue workers and police search for survivors after a recent hurricane flooded the streets of New Orleans.

TRAINING TO RESPOND

When disaster strikes, first responders are the first to arrive on the scene. They are also the last to leave a disaster area. First responders put their own lives at risk every time they respond to an emergency. They never know what to expect until they reach the affected area. Proper training in skills such as rescue techniques is very important.

First responders who work on land include police officers, firefighters, search-and-rescue teams, emergency medical technicians (EMTs), and communications experts. They are all trained to take control of a crisis. They often have to work together to get help to people in need. They make the environment safe again for the people who live there.

First responders can be volunteers or paid employees. In small towns, emergency service personnel and firefighters are usually volunteers from the community. In larger cities, these people get paid to do their jobs. They choose these careers because they want to help others. Both volunteers and paid workers know that they offer an important service. They also know that they have a huge responsibility. People are depending on them for help in dangerous situations.

FIREFIGHTERS

In the United States there are about one million firefighters. Firefighters are usually the first on the scene when disaster strikes. Firefighters are trained to put out fires and save people from fires. A firefighter goes through a lot of difficult training. A person who wants to become a firefighter must pass a series of incredibly difficult psychological, physical, and intellectual tests. Many people who start the training do not finish it.

Firefighters must be quick thinkers. Often, they have very little time to make life or death decisions. They must be prepared to go into dark buildings filled with hot, thick smoke and falling debris. They risk their health and lives every time they battle a fire.

A New Orleans firefighter rescues a young girl during the aftermath of Hurricane Katrina.

POLICE OFFICERS

When disaster strikes, police officers have the very difficult job of maintaining order at the disaster scene. They are there to protect people and property. Also, a police officer may have to perform first aid, rescue people from trapped vehicles or buildings, and direct traffic away from danger.

Men and women who want to become police officers must attend a police academy for twelve to fourteen weeks. They are trained in the use of firearms, self-defense, and first aid. They are also trained to respond in disaster situations. Some police officers even choose to specialize in emergency response.

After a successful rescue operation, police rush a hurricane victim to safety.

All police officer trainees must pass physical training tests. They must also pass tough written exams. These exams test a trainee's knowledge of the law. New police officers also go through a long interview process with senior officers. The interviewers judge the new officers' ability to be honest, responsible, and make fair decisions.

EMTS AND PARAMEDICS

EMTs and paramedics need formal training to do their job. They must take courses and pass a test to become licensed. EMTs and paramedics are trained to treat a patient until they can get him or her to the hospital. They learn how to perform first aid at the scene of an accident or disaster to save someone's life.

Paramedics have more training than EMTs and can perform more medical procedures. EMTs and paramedics must know how to perform cardiopulmonary resuscitation (CPR) and administer medicine. Their training includes learning how to use medical equipment and how to handle an injured patient. They have

Paramedics help a critically ill patient onto a coast guard helicopter that will fly her to a hospital.

to be very careful when lifting and moving a patient. They do not want to further hurt an injured person. EMTs and paramedics must also be in good physical shape. They have to be strong enough to lift a patient onto a stretcher. The Department of Homeland Security reports that there are over 155,000 EMT workers in the United States.

TAKING CARE OF THEMSELVES

Many first responders have unusual working hours. They must be on call and ready 24 hours a day. Some first responders work the night shift. Others work during the day. During a disaster, first responders often have to stay on the job longer than usual. This can mean going a long time without sleep. If they become overworked or overstressed, however, first responders will not be able to do their job well.

First responder teams are on call twenty-four hours a day. Here, firefighters in Texas examine a map while battling a wildfire in 2005.

In Arlington, Virginia, volunteers pretend to be injured as part of a firefighters' training exercise.

First responders often witness horrific events. They deal with major tragedies and help injured and dying people. This can take a toll on their mental well-being. They must be in good physical and mental health. That means maintaining a healthy diet and getting a lot of exercise are very important. A first responder must be aware of his or her own limitations and avoid overworking.

DID YOU KNOW?

There are over eleven million state and local first responders in the United States. They all have very important jobs in their community. Many of these are volunteers who do not get paid for their hard work.

First responders roam a devastated New Orleans neighborhood in search of more hurricane victims.

chapter 2

TO THE RESCUE

First responders must be prepared for anything. This means remaining calm no matter what happens. First responders look around the scene to see who needs the most help. They must make sure the affected area is safe and secure. They do not want to get hurt while trying to help others.

FAST THINKING

EMTs and paramedics work closely with the police departments and firefighters during a crisis. EMTs and paramedics get to the victims in need as fast as possible. They use ambulances as traveling hospitals to provide medical help. They have to decide quickly what the best treatment is for the patient. During a disaster, this can depend on a lot of things. For example, there may be a lot of people who need emergency medical care. The EMTs and paramedics have to decide who needs treatment first. They also may not be able to get to a hospital right away, so they have to provide the victims with the best possible treatment on the spot.

EMTs also must decide what kind of assistance they will need. This can mean calling for backup. They will call their dispatcher to ask for help from other EMTs, firemen, or police. They may even call for helicopters to airlift people out of an area.

After a big disaster, EMTs and paramedics might have to set up a triage center. In a triage center, people are treated for injuries on the spot, starting with the more severe injuries. During Hurricane Katrina, triage centers were set up at New Orleans International Airport and other locations.

RESPONDING TO THE INJURED

EMTs and paramedics use special equipment, such as stomach pumps and oxygen tanks. They use defibrillators to restart patients' hearts if they have stopped. They apply different types of medicine and bandages. These first responders must be able to give medicine by injection.

Houston paramedics give medical attention to a woman.

EMTs and paramedics must make sure their ambulances always have the proper supplies. Ambulances are equipped with backboards and stretchers for carrying patients. They must also be cleaned after every patient, so that infections are not spread to others.

FIREFIGHTERS' TOOLS

Firefighters arrive on the scene already wearing protective clothing. Their clothing protects

Chemical terrorism, victim rescue, and crowd control are just some of the emergencies for which first responders must be prepared.

them from fire, extreme heat, and dangerous chemicals. Firefighters carry a Self-Contained Breathing Apparatus (SCBA). SCBA allows them to breathe in areas that are toxic, too dusty, or smoke filled.

Firefighters use different tools to get into burning buildings. They use axes to break windows or open doors. A Halligan is a long tool with a hook that is used to force open doors. The K-12 is a large saw used to cut holes in roofs. Fire trucks have tall ladders to reach people trapped in high places.

JAWS OF LIFE

A Hurst tool, also called the Jaws of Life, is used to open car doors to rescue trapped victims. It is also used to rip open the top of a car and move heavy debris. Police and firefighters use the Hurst tool in their work.

THE SEARCH IS ON

First responders rescue people in many ways. Sometimes the safest way to find a trapped person is to dig by hand. This is because heavy machinery can be very dangerous if the person's location is not certain. When a building collapses, hundreds of people might start digging through the rubble looking for survivors. Construction workers may help remove debris. Utility workers

Using dogs to help with search-and-rescue operations is a vital part of first response efforts

DID YOU KNOW?

The Army National Guard may be called in to assist in emergency situations. They provide security, medical assistance, transportation, and other support. They will sometimes be notified before a disaster such as a hurricane hits. This way they are ready to go as soon as possible.

quickly begin repairing damaged phone lines and power lines. This makes communication easier.

Rescue dogs are very important in search-and-rescue efforts. Sometimes they can find victims faster than their human counterparts. This is because dogs can smell a human being from up to 1 mile (1.6 km) away. Rescue dogs are trained to find people buried in rubble. They sniff around until they find a trapped person. Then they will bark to alert their handler. They may even tap the area with their paw to show where the person is.

FEMA can fulfill requests that local governments cannot, such as using military helicopters to airlift hurricane survivors.

Local first responders cannot always do their job alone. When disaster strikes, they may not have all the resources they need to help their community. This is when other agencies, such as the Federal Emergency Management Agency (FEMA), step in to help.

FEDERAL EMERGENCY MANAGEMENT AGENCY

FEMA is a government agency that assists communities during times of disaster. Sometimes a disaster is too big for state and local officials to handle on their own. This is when FEMA is called in. FEMA's goal is to save lives, protect property, and coordinate disaster operations. As early as 1803, the U.S. Congress began to pass laws to help victims of disasters. By the 1930s, the federal government began to provide money to rebuild places hit by natural disasters. Different government agencies were responsible for specific areas of rebuilding. For example, the Army Corps of Engineers was responsible for flood control and recovery projects. The Bureau of Public Roads was responsible for fixing highways and bridges. At times there was confusion about which agency was responsible for certain jobs. Congress

FEMA workers load thousands of instant meals onto a military aircraft that will transport the food to those who need it most.

wanted the agencies to work together. The U.S. president was given the responsibility of coordinating disaster relief.

By 1979, President Jimmy Carter helped put together FEMA to assume responsibility for disaster relief. The agency faced many natural disasters in its first few years. This included massive water contamination and a nuclear power plant accident. Over the years, FEMA has worked to make disaster response quicker and easier.

Due to the terrorist attack in New York City on September 11, 2001, FEMA was made part of the Department of Homeland Security in 2003. FEMA had to make sure that first responders were prepared in case of a terrorist attack.

FEMA STEPS IN

Today, FEMA has twenty-five hundred full-time employees. There are also five thousand part-time employees who are called in when there is a disaster. FEMA helps local and state first responders get the equipment needed in a disaster. They also help get relief efforts started

DID YOU KNOW?

The worst hurricane disaster in the United States was in 1900, when six thousand people died in a hurricane that hit Galveston, Texas.

at a disaster site. This includes setting up command centers where first responders can get information. FEMA provides food, water, and medical supplies at the disaster site. FEMA also helps local communities by preparing them for disasters before they happen. FEMA has training programs for state and local first responders.

Getting help from FEMA is not a simple process. The governor of a state must write a letter to the U.S. government asking for help. He or she must explain what kind of aid the state is hoping to receive. This can delay assistance. Sometimes, the governor of the state knows that a hurricane is on the way. He or she may choose to ask for assistance before disaster strikes. This way, FEMA is already prepared to help.

FEMA often works alongside other government agencies and organizations such as the **U.S. Navy and the Department of Defense.**

THE RED CROSS

In 1859, Henry Dunant, a Swiss man, organized people to help soldiers in the Battle of Solferino in Italy. Dunant then called for the creation of relief societies. In time the International Red Cross was formed. Today, the organization is known as the International Federation of Red Cross and Red Crescent Societies. Many countries around the world participate in the programs.

A SLOW RESPONSE

Hurricane Katrina hit the Gulf Coast on August 28, 2005. The governor of Louisiana, Kathleen Blanco, declared a state of emergency. The hurricane was approaching New Orleans with 127-mile-per-hour (204 kph) winds. The winds caused waters to surge, breaking the levees, or dams, resulting in major floods in New Orleans. The winds also destroyed many buildings and properties.

There were not enough state and local first responders to handle the emergencies that followed the hurricane. New Orleans and the surrounding areas needed help quickly. FEMA did not respond quickly enough. Local officials felt there was a lack of leadership in the federal government. Thousands of people were stranded throughout the city. They had no food or water.

Almost one week passed before help arrived from FEMA. Many people felt that the director of FEMA, Michael Brown, did not do his job. Eventually, Brown resigned from his position.

In 1887, Clara Barton founded the American Red Cross in the United States. She modeled the agency after the International Red Cross. The goal of the Red Cross is to save lives and ease suffering. The American Red Cross provides help during emergencies such as natural disasters. This organization depends on donations from the public to support itself. Most Red Cross workers are volunteers. They can be at disaster sites in as little as two hours after disaster strikes. The Red Cross provides relief to victims of disasters. They also prepare people for future emergencies.

ON THE SCENE

In times of disaster, the Red Cross and Red Crescent provide food, shelter, and health services to those in need. They may also help victims pay for groceries, clothing, medications, and emergency repairs.

The agency has trained over eleven million people in life-saving skills worldwide. Their trained disaster specialists are always on call in case of an emergency. They respond to house fires, floods, hurricanes, earthquakes, tornadoes, explosions, and other natural and manmade disasters.

The Red Cross and Red Crescent also take care of the first responders. The first responders must have food to eat and a place to stay. In addition, the Red Cross and Red Crescent provide mental health services to both victims of a disaster and first responders. They know that talking about their feelings helps people get through bad situations.

DID YOU KNOW?

In countries where most of the citizens are Muslim, the image of a red crescent is used to represent the Red Cross and Red Crescent Societies.

A **Red Cross** worker delivers sandwiches as part of a major relief effort for victims of **Hurricane Katrina**.

Every year, the **Red Cross** aids thousands of people who find themselves displaced from their homes by natural disasters.

chapter 4

PLANNING FOR EMERGENCIES

First responders are constantly working to improve disaster relief efforts. They continually analyze their rescue plans for effectiveness. First responders also try to work with the best equipment possible. New and improved technology can help save lives during a disaster. Even a simple advance in administering a drug might save a life.

Equipment, however, can be expensive. First response organizations do not always have the money to get the latest and safest equipment. They often wait a long time before receiving aid from the federal government. This can mean they have to work without the proper gear.

COMMUNITY WORK

First responder organizations have set up goals to make sure people get the care they need during an emergency. One way they can do this is by putting life-saving equipment, such as defibrillators, in schools and on airplanes. This can save precious minutes in an emergency. Also, public outreach programs have been put into place around the country to educate people on what to do in case of emergencies. First responders hope that community members will get involved and learn how to protect themselves.

First responders face other challenges as well. They are trained to deal with various reactions from people they are trying to help. For example, children might be fearful of them and refuse to listen to instructions. Some people might not understand a first responder's offer to help. These people may be the elderly, people who speak a different language, or mentally ill people. First responders must be patient and understanding during a crisis.

A NEW KIND OF DISASTER

Today, first responders are being trained to deal with terrorist attacks such as chemical warfare and large-scale bombings. This means that

EMTs and paramedics may soon be trained to carry certain antidotes. They will have to know how to give out these antidotes quickly to a large number of people.

First responders need to find a balance between preparing for possible terrorist attacks and training to deal with natural disasters. Some people feel that this was a problem when Hurricane Katrina hit. Many first responders felt that their training focused too much on terrorism and too little on natural disaster recovery. Also, a large percentage of the National Guard was overseas in Iraq during the hurricane. This meant fewer first responders were available on home soil when they were needed. These are issues that the Department of Homeland Security must face in the twenty-first century.

DID YOU KNOW?

The American Red Cross provides aid to over sixty thousand disaster victims each year in the United States.

AFTER A DISASTER

Places hit by a disaster may take years to recover. A tsunami hit Southeast Asia in 2004, causing much damage. Almost a year later, an earthquake destroyed areas of northern Pakistan. The rebuilding in those regions is still going on today. First responders often come from other countries and cities to help out. They put their skills to work in many ways.

HELPING ACROSS BORDERS

To help the victims of the 2005 earthquake in northern Pakistan, the Norwegian Red Cross Mountain Rescue Corps sent in volunteers and all-terrain vehicles (ATVs). The ATVs can move easily over snow, mud, and rocky land. People who need medical help can be transported in the ATVs. The volunteers provide supplies such as blankets, stoves, tools, and iron sheeting, which can be used in rebuilding homes.

They may help by providing people with counseling. Others may remove debris or help build new houses.

First responders have very stressful jobs. They put themselves in dangerous situations to help others to safety. Their job is also very rewarding. There is no better feeling than knowing you have helped another person and that you have truly made a difference.

A United Nations helicopter lands in Pakistan as survivors of the devastating 2005 earthquake try to recover from the catastrophe.

NEW WORDS

antidote (**an**-ti-dote) something that stops a poison from working

apparatus (ap-uh-**rat**-uhss) equipment used to do a job

contamination (kuhn-tam-uh-**nay**-shuhn) pollution

crescent (**kress**-uhnt) a curved shape, like a quarter moon

crowbar (**kroh**-bar) a heavy steel or iron bar used to lift things or pry something open

debris (duh-**bree**) the scattered pieces of something that has been broken or destroyed

defibrillator (dee-**fih**-bruh-lay-tuhr) a device that applies electric shocks to the heart to help it start working again

devastation (**dev**-uh-stay-shuhn) the complete destruction of something

dispatcher (diss-**pach**-ur) a person who sends first responders out on rescue assignments

emergency (ih-**mur**-juhn-see) a sudden and dangerous situation that must be dealt with quickly

engineer (en-juh-**nihr**) someone who is trained to design and build things such as bridges, buildings, and machines

NEW WORDS

evacuation (i-**vak**-yoo-ay-shun) when people leave an area because there is danger

firearms (**fire**-armz) weapons that shoot bullets

intellectual (in-tuh-**lek**-choo-uhl) involving thought and reason

international (in-tur-**nash**-uh-nuhl) involving different countries

levees (**lev**-eez) banks built up near a river to prevent flooding

limitations (lim-uh-**tay**-shuhnz) points beyond which someone cannot or should not go

Muslims (**muhz**-limz) people who follow the religion of Islam, a religion based on the teachings of Muhammad

terrain (tuh-**rayn**) ground or land

triage center (**tree**-age **sen**-tur) a place set up to treat patients during emergency situations

tsunami (tsoo-**nah**-mee) a series of very large, destructive waves caused by an underwater earthquake or volcano

volunteers (vol-uhn-**tihrz**) people who offer to do a job, usually without pay

FOR FURTHER READING

Binns, Tristan Boyer. *FEMA: Federal Emergency Management Agency.* Portsmouth, NH: Heinemann, 2003.

Burger, Leslie. *Red Cross, Red Crescent: When Help Can't Wait.* Minneapolis, MN: Lerner Publications, 1996.

Thompson, Tamara. *Emergency Response.* San Diego: CA: Lucent Books, 2004.

Torr, James. *Responding to Attack: Firefighters and Police.* San Diego, CA: Lucent Books, 2003.

Raatma, Lucia. *Safety During Emergencies.* Chanhassen, MN: Child's World Inc., 2003.

ORGANIZATIONS

American Red Cross National Headquarters
2025 E Street, NW
Washington, DC 20006
(202) 303-4498
www.redcross.org

FEMA: Federal Emergency Management Agency
500 C Street, SW
Washington, DC 20472
1-800-621-FEMA (3362)
www.fema.gov

RESOURCES

WEB SITES

Emergency Medical Technicians and Paramedics
www.bls.gov/oco/ocos101.htm
Interested in finding out more about what paramedics and EMTs do? There is plenty of information on the type of work that these first responders do as well as how much they earn.

Fact Monster: History of Fire Fighting
www.factmonster.com/ce6/sci/A0858120.html
Read all about the history of fire fighting on this Web site.

FBI Working Dogs
www.fbi.gov/kids/dogs/doghome.htm
Explore this site to find out about search-and-rescue dogs or other working dogs.

Test of Courage
www.pbs.org/testofcourage
This Web site offers an inside look at the lives of firefighters and the kind of challenges they face.

INDEX

INDEX

ABOUT THE AUTHOR

Aileen Weintraub is a freelance author and editor living in the scenic Hudson Valley in upstate New York. She has authored over forty-five books for children and young adults. She also writes for a variety of newspapers and magazines.